LONGING FOR COMPANY
6 STUDIES FOR WOMEN ON LONELINESS

DR. JUDY HAMLIN

A DIVISION OF SCRIPTURE PRESS PUBLICATIONS INC.
USA CANADA ENGLAND

Scripture quotations are from the Holy Bible, New International Version®. Copyright © 1973, 1978, 1984 by International Bible Society. Used by permission of Zondervan Publishing House. All rights reserved.

Copyediting: Jane Vogel
Cover Design: Scott Rattray
Cover Illustration: Robert Bergin
Interior Illustrations: Al Hering

Recommended Dewey Decimal Classification: 243.833
Suggested Subject Heading: BIBLE STUDY: WOMEN
Library of Congress Catalog Card Number: 93-29170
ISBN: 1-56476-195-9

1 2 3 4 5 6 7 8 9 10 Printing/Year 97 96 95 94 93

© 1993 by Victor Books/SP Publications, Inc. All rights reserved. Printed in the United States of America. No part of this book may be reproduced without written permission, except for brief quotations in books, critical articles, and reviews.

VICTOR BOOKS
A division of SP Publications, Inc.
Wheaton, Illinois 60187

CONTENTS

Introduction **5**

1. *How Am I Lonely? Let Me Count the Ways* **7**
2. *Alone in a Crowd* **15**
3. *Overcoming Versus Withdrawing* **21**
4. *Alone but Not Lonely* **29**
5. *Lonely Places* **35**
6. *Getting by with a Little Help from My Friend* **43**

Leader's Notes **47**
Five Steps **64**

To Terry Ronning, a friend who is able to overlook my faults and accept me with my warts and growls, and who comforts me when loneliness rears its head.

INTRODUCTION

Loneliness strikes everyone and every age. It is not a new topic for study. Being prepared to handle loneliness is the issue. If we know what loneliness is, what it isn't, what causes it, and how to acknowledge it, we can take action to overcome it. At some point, we'll also be prepared to help others.

In this study we will respond to loneliness in a positive way. We'll learn to prepare for inevitable loneliness, and to distinguish between loneliness and simply being lonely.

Each session in this study includes:
- ☐ *Scripture* and *Purpose* statements that reflect the goals of the session.
- ☐ *Looking Inside*, combining questions with illustrations to be used as conversation starters.
- ☐ *Topical Text* that prompts participants to work through specific issues.
- ☐ *Scriptures* that speak to those specific issues.
- ☐ *Praying Together*, which encourages participants to develop the discipline of prayer and praise.

In the *Leader's Notes* you will find background information, additional questions, and an outline for each session. During the course of this study the Holy Spirit might prompt you to make a decision to receive Jesus Christ as your Lord and Savior. If this happens, turn to the back of the study and review the Five Steps. You may do this alone, with a friend, or with your group leader. Record your spiritual birthday, then read, claim, and receive God's gifts.

How Am I Lonely? Let Me Count the Ways

SCRIPTURE
"Turn to me and be gracious to me, for I am lonely and afflicted" *(Psalm 25:16)*.

PURPOSE
To describe different types of loneliness and show how we can grow through them.

LOOKING INSIDE
1. Which of the following song lyrics best reflects the fact for you that loneliness affects children, teenagers, middle-aged adults, elderly persons—in fact, each of us?

   ☐ "Look at all those lonely people. Where do they all come from?"
   ☐ "Sometimes I feel like a motherless child, a long way from home."
   ☐ "Alone again, naturally."
   ☐ "Love lifted me, love lifted me; when nothing else would do, love lifted me."

2. Which song lyric best reflects a lonely experience you have faced recently?

3. Which best describes how you would like to feel about loneliness?

8 LONGING FOR COMPANY

AN EPIDEMIC

Loneliness has become epidemic in America, a nearly permanent condition for millions. Everyone is lonely at times, but many are lonely most of the time. It has been said that 3 billion people around the world go to bed hungry every night, but 4 billion go to bed needing love and attention.

Lonely people include: (1) rising executives who no longer talk with their spouses; (2) young single adults living alone for the first time in big city apartment complexes; (3) older singles giving up hope of finding companionship; (4) widowers and widows trying to cope with the loss of spouses; (5) homemakers surrounded all day by preschoolers; (6) couples who have moved for the third time in two years; and (7) those experiencing divorce or separation.

People experience different types of loneliness: "circumstantial," "chosen," "self-protective," and "inner-core." Which of the people listed above would you say experience:

"circumstantial" loneliness?

"chosen" loneliness?

"self-protective" loneliness?

"inner-core" loneliness?

LONELINESS DEFINED

Let's consider a definition of loneliness. Check all the statements you think describe loneliness.

- [ ] An inner longing for completeness.
- [ ] Being by oneself.
- [ ] Feeling alone.
- [ ] An unsatisfied desire for companionship.
- [ ] An unsatisfied desire for belonging.
- [ ] An unsatisfied desire for approval.

CATEGORIES OF LONELINESS

Recall experiences you have had with loneliness, and people you know who are lonely. In which of the following four categories would you place those experiences and people? Give first names and brief descriptions.

Category 1: Loneliness created by other people or circumstances.

Category 2: Loneliness as a choice of the individual.

Category 3: Self-protective loneliness.

Category 4: Inner-core loneliness.

As a group, tally the number of entries for each category. Which category has the most entries?

Category 1 Circumstantial	Category 2 Chosen	Category 3 Self-protective	Category 4 Inner-core

10 LONGING FOR COMPANY

BIBLICAL EXAMPLES
Let's look at some examples of "lonely people" in the Bible and how they handled their feelings.

1. As you read the following passages from the Psalms, describe David's response as he flees the King's wrath and experiences extreme periods of loneliness. Where is David's hope?

> My God, my God, why have You forsaken me?
> Why are You so far from saving me, so far from the words of my groaning?
> O my God, I cry out by day, but You do not answer, by night, and am not silent.
> Yet You are enthroned as the Holy One; You are the praise of Israel.
> In You our fathers put their trust; they trusted and You delivered them.
> They cried to You and were saved; in You they trusted and were not disappointed.
> But I am a worm and not a man, scorned by men and despised by the people.
> All who see me mock me; they hurl insults, shaking their heads:
> "He trusts in the LORD; let the LORD rescue him.
> Let Him deliver him, since he delights in Him."
> Yet You brought me out of the womb; You made me trust in You even at my mother's breast.
> From birth I was cast upon You; from my mother's womb
> You have been my God. Do not be far from me, for trouble is near and there is no one to help *(Psalm 22:1-11).*

> Turn to me and be gracious to me, for I am lonely and afflicted.
> The troubles of my heart have multiplied; free me from my anguish.
> Look upon my affliction and my distress and take away all my sins.
> See how my enemies have increased and how fiercely they hate me!
> Guard my life and rescue me; let me not be put to shame, for I take refuge in You *(Psalm 25:16-20).*

> In my alarm I said, "I am cut off from Your sight!"
> Yet You heard my cry for mercy when I called to You for help.
> Love the LORD, all His saints! The LORD preserves the faithful, but the proud He pays back in full. Be strong and take heart, all you who hope in the LORD *(Psalm 31:22-24).*

> You have made my days a mere handbreadth;
>   the span of my years is as nothing before You.
> Each man's life is but a breath.
> Selah
> Man is a mere phantom as he goes to and fro:
> He bustles about, but only in vain;
>   he heaps up wealth, not knowing who will get it.
> But now, Lord, what do I look for? My hope is in You
> *(Psalm 39:5-7).*

2. The author of Hebrews seemed to be lonely. What comfort did he find and what gave him the ability to say these words?

> Keep your lives free from the love of money and be content with what you have, because God has said, "Never will I leave you; never will I forsake you." So we say with confidence, "The Lord is my helper; I will not be afraid. What can man do to me?" *(Hebrews 13:5-6)*

3. The Apostle Paul knew what it is like to be driven out of a city or thrown in jail for his beliefs. Yet after years of such treatment, he was able to make one of the most profound declarations in Scripture. In your own words describe what he wrote in Philippians 4:11-13.

> I am not saying this because I am in need, for I have learned to be content whatever the circumstances. I know

12 LONGING FOR COMPANY

what it is to be in need, and I know what it is to have plenty. I have learned the secret of being content in any and every situation, whether well fed or hungry, whether living in plenty or in want. I can do everything through Him who gives me strength *(Philippians 4:11-13).*

4. Ultimately David reaped great benefits from his times of loneliness and affliction. What does he say he learned?

> Do good to Your servant, and I will live; I will obey Your word *(Psalm 119:17).*

> Your word is a lamp to my feet and a light for my path *(Psalm 119:105).*

5. A doctor once told his patient, "Ma'am, your troubles is nothin' but aggravated selfishness." He sent her out to be a volunteer. She followed his advice and found a cure for all her "imagined" ills. What does God promise volunteeers in Isaiah 58:10-12?

> If you spend yourselves in behalf of the hungry and satisfy the needs of the oppressed, then your light will rise in the darkness, and your night will become like the noonday. The LORD will guide you always; He will satisfy your needs in a sun-scorched land and will strengthen your frame. You will be like a well-watered garden, like a spring whose waters never fail. Your people will rebuild the ancient ruins and will raise up the age-old foundations; you will be called Repairer of Broken Walls, Restorer of Streets with Dwellings *(Isaiah 58:10-12).*

How would this advice help lonely people?

TAKE FIVE
Select one of these examples of loneliness and discuss with your neighbor what counsel you would give the person if he or she asked you for help in overcoming loneliness.

- ☐ A single adult alone for the first time in a large city.
- ☐ A homemaker/mother caring for a preschooler.
- ☐ A widow/widower trying to cope with spousal loss.
- ☐ A young married couple new to a city.
- ☐ A recently divorced or separated woman.
- ☐ A rising executive who no longer talks to her spouse.
- ☐ An older woman who's given up trying to make friends.

PRAYING TOGETHER
Choose the prayer that best fits your need today, fill in the blank(s), and pray it during the group prayer time.

Father, I know You're with _____ in this crisis. Bring her safely through surgery.

You know my needs before I do, Lord. I pray that Your will be done.

As You have blessed me so greatly, please let my bounty glorify You.

Dear Lord, be close to _____ as her child struggles in rebellion.

_____ is new to the city, Father. Let Your spirit comfort her in all her new situations.

THIS WEEK
Read and reflect on Psalm 139:1-24. Next week be prepared to share lonely moments and how you handled them.

ALONE IN A CROWD

SCRIPTURE
"When I am afraid, I will trust in You. In God, whose word I praise, in God I trust; I will not be afraid. What can mortal man do to me?" *(Psalm 56:3-4)*

PURPOSE
To observe how others can affect a person's loneliness.

LOOKING INSIDE
1. When you are feeling lonely, what would you like for someone else to say or do for you?

2. What does this song line say to you about shared loneliness?

"Only the lonely know the heartache I've been through."

3. Have you known someone who was lonely? How did you respond?

STRESSORS
A "stressor" is an event, occurrence, person, irritant, thought, or memory that causes unhealthy stress. Stressors are present in

16 LONGING FOR COMPANY

each of our lives. It's how we handle them that differs. Of course, while we are required to overcome them on a daily basis, other people can impact how we handle them.

On a scale of 10 to 100 (100 being highest [something you experience most of the time] and 10 lowest [something you never experience]), rank yourself on how well you handle the following stressors.

ACTIVITIES	STRESS FACTORS
Feeling disconnected	
A sense of worthlessness	
Isolation	
Allowing others to confirm rejection	
Difficulty making friends	
Bitterness	
Self-pity	
Feeling you have lost respect of others	
Loss of loved one, friends, or job	
Changing locations	
An unclear perspective	
Priorities out of balance	
Fear	

After you have ranked each activity, identify the three highest and lowest.

ALONE IN A CROWD   17

#1 highest: #1 lowest:

#2 highest: #2 lowest:

#3 highest: #3 lowest:

BIBLICAL "OTHERS"

The authors of the following Scriptures felt lonely for different reasons. Read each, then discuss what others are doing to create feelings of loneliness.

"All day long my enemies taunt me; those who rail against me use my name as a curse" *(Psalm 102:8).*

"You have taken from me my closest friends and have made me repulsive to them. I am confined and cannot escape" *(Psalm 88:8).*

"At my first defense, no one came to my support, but everyone deserted me. May it not be held against them" *(2 Timothy 4:16).*

" 'But this has all taken place that the writings of the prophets might be fulfilled.' Then all the disciples deserted Him and fled" *(Matthew 26:56).*

RESPONDING IN LOVE

> "SO IN EVERYTHING, DO TO OTHERS WHAT YOU WOULD HAVE THEM DO TO YOU, FOR THIS SUMS UP THE LAW AND THE PROPHETS" *(Matthew 7:12).*

18 LONGING FOR COMPANY

Because we hurt so deeply when we are lonely, we tend to lash out at others. Scripture can help guide us during such a time. Discuss the questions in light of the Scriptures that follow.

1. In what specific ways and situations can we avoid being judgmental of others?

   Do not judge, or you too will be judged. For in the same way you judge others, you will be judged, and with the measure you use, it will be measured to you *(Matthew 7:1-2)*.

2. When someone reaches out to you, how can you express gratitude? How do you react when someone fails to express gratitude to you?

   In Luke's account of Jesus' healing ten lepers we are told that only one came back to thank Jesus. Jesus asked, "Were not all ten cleansed? Where are the other nine?" *(Luke 17:17)*

3. How can we learn to accept criticism without taking offense?

   Whatever you do, work at it with all your heart, as working for the Lord, not for men, since you know that you will receive an inheritance from the Lord as a reward. It is the Lord Christ you are serving. Anyone who does wrong will be repaid for his wrong, and there is no favoritism *(Colossians 3:23-25)*.

4. What are some specific ways to help others feel significant?

   Do nothing out of selfish ambition or vain conceit, but in humility consider others better than yourselves. Each of you should look not only to your own interests, but also to the interests of others *(Philippians 2:3-4)*.

ALONE IN A CROWD 19

5. How well do you accept and love yourself?

> The second [greatest commandment] is this: "Love your neighbor as yourself." There is no commandment greater than these *(Mark 12:31)*.

6. What difficult circumstances must you accept and deal with right now?

> Do everything without complaining or arguing *(Philippians 2:14)*.

PRAYING TOGETHER
Choose the prayer that best fits your need today, fill in the blank(s), and pray the sentence during the group prayer time.

Father, thank You for giving me confidence to face my trials.

Give _____ faith that You are in control even when circumstances seem out of control.

Dear God, help me accept Your grace and peace as I deal with the stress of my job.

Thank you, Lord, for the chance to help my sister while she was in the hospital.

Give me the wisdom, Father, to always seek Your will when I face my difficult decisions.

THIS WEEK
Use God's telephone number (Jeremiah 33:3) and call out in prayer whenever other people inflict hurt, pain, or anguish or take any action that causes you to feel lonely.

"Call to Me and I will answer you and tell you great and unsearchable things you do not know" *(Jeremiah 33:3)*.

OVERCOMING VERSUS WITHDRAWING

SCRIPTURE
"But Jesus immediately said to them: 'Take courage! It is I. Don't be afraid' " *(Matthew 14:27).*

PURPOSE
To explore how to acknowledge our loneliness and let God work through it.

LOOKING INSIDE
1. Which of these song lyrics best describes your feelings of loneliness?

   ☐ "Sometimes I feel like a motherless child, a long way from home."
   ☐ "One less bell to answer, one less egg to fry."
   ☐ "All dressed up with nowhere to go."
   ☐ "At seventeen."

2. Describe a time of day or year when you feel most lonely.

3. Do you think most country music is sad and reflects loneliness? Explain.

FEELINGS IDENTIFIED
"If only I hadn't changed jobs. If only a past relationship had not been severed. If only we hadn't moved again. If only I could get away from the kids. If only...." Complete the following "if only" statements to show how you feel. Be honest with yourself.

If only . . .

If only . . .

If only . . .

If only . . .

This is how Jesus responded to a would-be follower who wanted to go home and say good-bye: "No one who puts his hand to the plow and looks back is fit for service in the kingdom of God" (Luke 9:62). This tells us that our focus is not to be on yesterday, but rather on the road God has placed before us. We are not to continually look back.

OVERCOMING LONELINESS
To overcome feelings of loneliness, we must first
> Acknowledge our loneliness; then
> Accept it;
> Act to overcome it; and
> Above all, help others.

Discuss the following questions.

> Do I really want out of my loneliness?
>
> Does the expression on my face show my thoughts of isolation?
>
> Am I unnecessarily afraid of people?
>
> If so, why am I afraid of them?
>
> Do I believe God can help solve my loneliness problem?
>
> Am I willing to be hurt to love others?
>
> What is it I'm trying to protect by withdrawing? Is it working? What are the consequences?
>
> (Dawson McAllister. *Dawson speaks out on . . . Self-Esteem and Loneliness,* Shepherd Ministries, 1989, p. 27.)

WHEN GOD BRINGS GOOD OUT OF LONELINESS
Many biblical figures faced loneliness. Let's consider three episodes.

1. Joseph

> So when Joseph came to his brothers, they stripped him of his robe—the richly ornamented robe he was wearing—and they took him and threw him into the cistern. Now the cistern was empty; there was no water in it.
>
> As they sat down to eat their meal, they looked up and saw a caravan of Ishmaelites coming from Gilead. Their camels were loaded with spices, balm and myrrh, and they were on their way to take them down to Egypt.
>
> Judah said to his brothers, "What will we gain if we kill our brother and cover up his blood? Come, let's sell him to the Ishmaelites and not lay our hands on him; after all, he is our brother, our own flesh and blood." His brothers agreed.
>
> So when the Midianite merchants came by, his brothers pulled Joseph up out of the cistern and sold him for twenty shekels of silver to the Ishmaelites, who took him to Egypt *(Genesis 37:23-28).*

How would you have felt in Joseph's situation?

Let the group leader or someone in the group summarize the rest of Joseph's story. In what instances did Joseph choose to act when he could have chosen to withdraw?

What good did God bring out of Joseph's lonely situation?

2. Ruth

When she heard in Moab that the LORD had come to the aid of His people by providing food for them, Naomi and her daughters-in-law prepared to return home from there. With her two daughters-in-law she left the place where she had been living and set out on the road that would take them back to the land of Judah.

Then Naomi said to her two daughters-in-law, "Go back, each of you, to your mother's home. May the LORD show kindness to you, as you have shown to your dead and to me. May the LORD grant that each of you will find rest in the home of another husband."

Then she kissed them and they wept aloud and said to her, "We will go back with you to your people."

But Naomi said, "Return home, my daughters. Why would you come with me? Am I going to have any more sons, who could become your husbands? Return home, my daughters; I am too old to have another husband. Even if I thought there was still hope for me—even if I had a husband tonight and then gave birth to sons—would you wait until they grew up? Would you remain unmarried for them? No, my daughters. It is more bitter for me than for you, because the LORD's hand has gone out against me!"

At this they wept again. Then Orpah kissed her mother-in-law good-by, but Ruth clung to her.

"Look," said Naomi, "your sister-in-law is going back to her people and her gods. Go back with her."

But Ruth replied, "Don't urge me to leave you or to turn back from you. Where you go I will go, and where you stay I will stay. Your people will be my people and your God my

God. Where you die I will die, and there I will be buried. May the LORD deal with me, be it ever so severely, if anything but death separates you and me." When Naomi realized that Ruth was determined to go with her, she stopped urging her.

So the two women went on until they came to Bethlehem. When they arrived in Bethlehem, the whole town was stirred because of them, and the women exclaimed, "Can this be Naomi?"

"Don't call me Naomi," she told them. "Call me Mara, because the Almighty has made my life very bitter. I went away full, but the LORD has brought me back empty. Why call me Naomi? The LORD has afflicted me; the Almighty has brought misfortune upon me."

So Naomi returned from Moab accompanied by Ruth the Moabitess, her daughter-in-law, arriving in Bethlehem as the barley harvest was beginning *(Ruth 1:6-22).*

If you had been Ruth, do you think you would have left your country and family to follow Naomi?

What factors do you suppose might make Ruth lonely in her new home?

Let the group leader or someone in the group summarize the rest of Ruth's story. In what instances did Ruth choose to act when she could have chosen to withdraw?

What good did God bring out of Ruth's lonely situation?

3. Mary and Joseph

> In those days Caesar Augustus issued a decree that a census should be taken of the entire Roman world. (This was the first census that took place while Quirinius was governor of Syria.) And everyone went to his own town to register.
>
> So Joseph also went up from the town of Nazareth in Galilee to Judea, to Bethlehem the town of David, because he belonged to the house and line of David. He went there to register with Mary, who was pledged to be married to him and was expecting a child *(Luke 2:1-5)*.

What would have made you feel lonely in Mary's situation? How do you suppose Joseph felt?

Let the group leader or someone in the group summarize the rest of Mary and Joseph's story. What good did God bring out of their lonely situation?

TAKE FIVE
Take time to visit with your neighbor. Can you think of a time when God overcame your loneliness to create something positive?

PRAYING TOGETHER
Take comfort in the following Scriptures. Read them together as you close your session.

> *"And we know that in all things God works for the good of those who love Him, who have been called according to His purpose. For those God foreknew He also predestined to be conformed to the likeness of His Son, that He might be the firstborn among many brothers" (Romans 8:28-29).*

"Who is he that condemns? Christ Jesus, who died—more than that, who was raised to life—is at the right hand of God and is also interceding for us. Who shall separate us from the love of Christ? Shall trouble or hardship or persecution or famine or nakedness or danger or sword? As it is written: 'For Your sake we face death all day long; we are considered as sheep to be slaughtered.' No, in all these things we are more than conquerors through Him who loved us. For I am convinced that neither death nor life, neither angels nor demons, neither the present nor the future, nor any powers, neither height nor depth, nor anything else in all creation, will be able to separate us from the love of God that is in Christ Jesus our Lord" (Romans 8:34-39).

THIS WEEK
If you find yourself lonely this week, select one of the following activities and respond to your loneliness.

- ☐ Read a good book.
- ☐ Call a friend.
- ☐ Write a letter.
- ☐ Complete a project you've started.
- ☐ Take someone to dinner.
- ☐ Go shopping.
- ☐ Volunteer at a retirement home.

ALONE BUT NOT LONELY

SCRIPTURE
"After He [Jesus] had dismissed them, He went up on a mountainside by Himself to pray. When evening came, He was there alone" *(Matthew 14:23)*.

PURPOSE
To define and evaluate time alone and its place in life.

LOOKING INSIDE
1. What is your fondest memory of being alone?

2. Select a song title from the list below and tell how you can relate to it.

- ☐ "Alone Again, Naturally"
- ☐ "Behind Closed Doors"
- ☐ "Life Has Its Little Ups and Downs"
- ☐ "Lonely at the Right Time"

3. Entering a restaurant and seeing a woman eating alone, do you feel sorry for her or think, "Good for her (you)"?

CREATING OPTIONS FOR TIME ALONE
Having quality time alone requires developing a list of options. Rate the following on how often you currently do each, then

how often you wish you could do each.

ACTIVITY	TIMES PER MONTH I CURRENTLY DO IT	TIMES PER MONTH I WOULD LIKE TO DO IT
Go to a movie		
Read a book		
Listen to lecture tapes		
Keep a journal		
Enjoy a hobby		
Browse magazines		
Rearrange a room		
Take a bubble bath		
Create a new recipe		
Play a favorite movie score		
Plant flowers in the yard		
Ignore the telephone		
Take a walk		
Write friends or family		
Clean a messy closet		
Study the Bible		
Spend time in prayer		
Go through a box of memorabilia		

List the three activities you most desire to do more often.

1.

2.

3.

TAKE FIVE
With your neighbor, discuss how you feel after spending time alone engaged in one of the activities you listed above, or how you think you would feel. How could you make more time for them?

BENEFITS OF TIME ALONE
The best way to handle time alone is to turn it from negative to positive. After all, approach and attitude are what made it negative in the first place. Dwell on benefits to be derived from time alone.

Read the following Scriptures, then complete the sentences focusing on what time alone allows you to do.

"Come to Me, all you who are weary and burdened, and I will give you rest" *(Matthew 11:28).*

Time alone allows . . .

"Teach me Your way, O LORD, and I will walk in Your truth; give me an undivided heart, that I may fear Your name" *(Psalm 86:11).*

Time alone allows . . .

"Pray in the Spirit on all occasions with all kinds of prayers and requests. With this in mind, be alert and always keep on praying for all the saints" *(Ephesians 6:18).*

Time alone allows . . .

"David was greatly distressed because the men were talking of stoning him; each one was bitter in spirit because of his sons and daughters. But David found strength in the LORD his God" *(1 Samuel 30:6).*

Time alone allows . . .

32 LONGING FOR COMPANY

"I am the vine; you are the branches. If a man remains in Me and I in him, he will bear much fruit; apart from Me you can do nothing" *(John 15:5).*

Time alone allows . . .

PRAYING TOGETHER

Choose a printed prayer or write your own to pray during the group prayer time.

When I'm alone, Father, let it lead to a closer relationship with You.

Since my husband died, Lord, I've learned that only You can take his place. Thank You for Your friendship.

It's remarkable how much I've learned to get done when I'm alone. Thank You, God.

Jesus, send Your Spirit to comfort _____ in the passing of her husband.

Lord, turn my mother's loneliness into a time of service to others.

THIS WEEK

Get to know yourself in time alone this week. Ask yourself the following questions and record your answers in a journal.

1. Are you using your spare time in a positive way? If not, how are you using it?

2. What social activities do you avoid or to which invitations do you say no? Evaluate why you say no.

Lonely Places

SCRIPTURE
"But Jesus often withdrew to lonely places and prayed" *(Luke 5:16)*.

PURPOSE
To identify those "lonely places" that must be accepted because they cannot be changed.

LOOKING INSIDE
1. Which song lyric or title reminds you of a lonely place you were in?

   ☐ "I come to the Garden alone."
   ☐ "MacArthur Park."
   ☐ "Jesus walked this lonesome valley."
   ☐ "Lonesome Town."

2. Who was with you there to comfort you?

3. What one lonely place in your life (isolation, sorrow, rejection, etc.) do you remember resulting in a positive experience?

LONELY THOUGHTS
When we think of lonely places, unusual settings come to mind: empty shopping malls, sparsely inhabited libraries, uncrowded doctors' waiting rooms. These seem lonely because they usually are filled with people and noise. The unexpected lack of people creates a void. An unexpected lonely place then becomes a

think tank, in which any number of positive or negative thoughts might emerge.

Take time now to add to the following list of thoughts which could surface.

LONELY THOUGHTS

- ☐ Sorrow
- ☐ Isolation
- ☐ Self-centeredness
- ☐ Risk I need to take
- ☐ Facing hard work
- ☐ How to pray
- ☐ Handling holidays
- ☐ Midlife issues
- ☐ Raising children
- ☐ Rejection
- ☐ An illness or pain
- ☐ What to do about physical and emotional tiredness
- ☐ How to get more rest
- ☐
- ☐
- ☐
- ☐
- ☐
- ☐
- ☐
- ☐

Take one of them—such as "handling holidays"—and create a list of ways to overcome the loneliness of it. For example: while sitting in the doctor's office create a list of things "to do" and to look forward to. Now you try it.

The lonely thought, feeling, event, etc.:

How I can overcome it:

LEAH'S LONELY PLACE

Genesis 29:20-35 tells the story of a woman in a lonely place.

Jacob had been sent to take Laban's daughter for a wife (Laban was his mother's brother). Once Jacob arrived at Laban's home, he met Rachel, the younger of two daughters, and fell in love with her. He offered to work for seven years for her hand in marriage. At the end of the seven years Laban gave Leah, the older daughter, to Jacob rather than Rachel.

When Jacob protested, Laban explained that custom required giving the older daughter first. Laban proposed that for seven more years' labor, Jacob could also have Rachel—but first he must complete a "honeymoon" week with Leah. Jacob did this and then married Rachel.

What do you think Leah might have been feeling during this time?

What did Leah need and want?

God's response is found in Genesis 29:31-35:

> When the LORD saw that Leah was not loved, He opened her womb, but Rachel was barren. Leah became pregnant and gave birth to a son. She named him Reuben, for she said, "It is because the LORD has seen my misery. Surely my husband will love me now."
>
> She conceived again, and when she gave birth to a son she said, "Because the LORD heard that I am not loved, He gave me this one too." So she named him Simeon.
>
> Again she conceived, and when she gave birth to a son she said, "Now at last my husband will become attached to me, because I have borne him three sons." So he was named Levi.

38 LONGING FOR COMPANY

> She conceived again, and when she gave birth to a son she said, "This time I will praise the Lord." So she named him Judah. Then she stopped having children *(Genesis 29:31-35)*.

Notice the change in Leah's response from her first son to her last. What do you think accounts for this difference?

TAKE FIVE
With your neighbor, discuss a lonely situation with which you are dealing. Have you accepted what you cannot change? Together, read Romans 8:28-29.

> And we know that in all things God works for the good of those who love Him, who have been called according to His purpose. For those God foreknew He also predestined to be conformed to the likeness of His Son, that He might be the firstborn among many brothers *(Romans 8:28-29)*.

What promises has God given to assure us that He knows what we are experiencing, that He recognizes where we are today, and that He has a purpose and plan for us?

OUR RESPONSE
How are we to respond or act in the midst of stress, loneliness, and change? Draw conclusions from the following Scriptures.

> "Noah did everything just as God commanded him" *(Genesis 6:22)*.

> "Be joyful always; pray continually; give thanks in all circumstances, for this is God's will for you in Christ Jesus" *(1 Thessalonians 5:16-18)*.

"Consider it pure joy, my brothers, whenever you face trials of many kinds, because you know that the testing of your faith develops perseverance. Perseverance must finish its work so that you may be mature and complete, not lacking anything" *(James 1:2-4).*

"Do not be anxious about anything, but in everything, by prayer and petition, with thanksgiving, present your requests to God" *(Philippians 4:6).*

"Finally, brothers, whatever is true, whatever is noble, whatever is right, whatever is pure, whatever is lovely, whatever is admirable—if anything is excellent or praiseworthy—think about such things" *(Philippians 4:8).*

PRAYING TOGETHER
Spend time in prayer together. Select one of the printed prayers or write your own.

Father, give me the strength to endure what I cannot change.

Dear Lord, be with me as I spend time thinking about _____ _____ and ways I can overcome the loneliness.

Father, I, like Leah, feel unloved. Make Your presence known to me. Comfort and help me.

Help me, Lord, to be obedient, to consider my trials joy, and not to be anxious.

Thank You, Father, for watching over my situation. I thank You for directing what is good for me.

THIS WEEK

Consider three items from the "Lonely Thoughts" list that occur in your life this week. When they occur, take a few minutes to pray for God's guidance; then make notes on things you can do to overcome, accept, and rejoice. Note whether the situation is something you can or cannot do anything about. Then read and claim God's promise in Romans 8:28.

"And we know that in all things God works for the good of those who love Him, who have been called according to His purpose" (Romans 8:28).

GETTING BY WITH A LITTLE HELP FROM MY FRIEND

SCRIPTURE
"God sets the lonely in families, He leads forth the prisoners with singing; but the rebellious live in a sun-scorched land" *(Psalm 68:6).*

PURPOSE
To establish that Jesus is a friend who cares for each individual, totally and unconditionally.

LOOKING INSIDE
1. Which of these song titles remind you of someone who cares for you so much that, no matter what happens, he or she will always listen and help?

    ☐ "Through the Years"
    ☐ "You Decorated My Life"
    ☐ "Since I fell For You"
    ☐ "Till I Can Make It on My Own"

2. Fill in the blank with the first name of someone with whom you are totally honest: _____ . What special character traits are evident in this person?

3. Whom do you care for in an unconditional way?

FRIENDS
Following are biblical examples of friends who reached out in times of need, sometimes facing danger and ridicule. Create a

list of their character traits, as they are revealed in Scripture.

1. Jonathan

> After David had finished talking with Saul, Jonathan became one in spirit with David, and he loved him as himself. From that day Saul kept David with him and did not let him return to his father's house. And Jonathan made a covenant with David because he loved him as himself. Jonathan took off the robe he was wearing and gave it to David, along with his tunic, and even his sword, his bow and his belt *(1 Samuel 18:1-4).*

Jonathan's character traits:

2. Four friends of the paralytic

> One day as He [Jesus] was teaching, Pharisees and teachers of the law, who had come from every village of Galilee and from Judea and Jerusalem, were sitting there. And the power of the Lord was present for Him to heal the sick. Some men came carrying a paralytic on a mat and tried to take him into the house to lay him before Jesus. When they could not find a way to do this because of the crowd, they went up on the roof and lowered him on his mat through the tiles into the middle of the crowd, right in front of Jesus *(Luke 5:17-19).*

Character traits of the four friends:

3. Mary

> Six days before the Passover, Jesus arrived at Bethany, where Lazarus lived, whom Jesus had raised from the dead. Here a dinner was given in Jesus' honor. Martha served, while Lazarus was among those reclining at the table with Him. Then Mary took about a pint of pure nard,

GETTING BY WITH A LITTLE HELP FROM MY FRIEND 45

an expensive perfume; she poured it on Jesus' feet and wiped His feet with her hair. And the house was filled with the fragrance of the perfume *(John 12:1-3).*

Mary's character traits:

THE ULTIMATE FRIEND
Look again at the list of character traits you identified, then jot down ways that Jesus exemplifies each of these traits.

Far beyond even the best of human friends, Jesus cares for the total person, whatever the need.

> While Jesus was in one of the towns, a man came along who was covered with leprosy. When he saw Jesus, he fell with his face to the ground and begged Him, "Lord, if You are willing, You can make me clean."
>
> Jesus reached out His hand and touched the man. "I am willing," He said. "Be clean!" And immediately the leprosy left him *(Luke 5:12-13).*

When the leper came to Jesus, he had no friends and was totally alone. Yet Jesus reached out to him. His response is always to deal with a person's basic need. What were the leper's basic needs?

How did Jesus meet those needs?

TAKE FIVE
With your neighbor, take five minutes to discuss the two most important needs in your life. Can these needs be seen or are

they hidden? How can Jesus meet them?

PRAYING TOGETHER
The following Scriptures contain many of God's promises. Your group leader will direct your prayer time using these Scriptures.

"He who did not spare His own Son, but gave Him up for us all — how will He not also, along with Him, graciously give us all things?" (Romans 8:32)

"And God is able to make all grace abound to you, so that in all things at all times, having all that you need, you will abound in every good work" (2 Corinthians 9:8).

"And my God will meet all your needs according to His glorious riches in Christ Jesus" (Philippians 4:19).

"For God so loved the world that He gave His one and only Son, that whoever believes in Him shall not perish but have eternal life" (John 3:16).

"But God demonstrates His own love for us in this: While we were still sinners, Christ died for us" (Romans 5:8).

"Now to Him who is able to do immeasurably more than all we ask or imagine, according to His power that is at work within us, to Him be glory in the church and in Christ Jesus throughout all generations, forever and ever! Amen" (Ephesians 3:20-21).

THIS WEEK
Often, when we need help, we refuse to accept it when offered. Have you asked Jesus to demonstrate His love and care for you by meeting a need in your life? Are you willing to accept His help? Is there anything that prevents you from asking?

Claim God's promises as you pray about your needs. Remember that Jesus promises, "I will never leave or forsake you" *(Hebrews 13:5).*

LEADER'S NOTES 1
HOW AM I LONELY? LET ME COUNT THE WAYS

WELCOME
Welcome each participant to the group. Point out that this study book provides Scripture, but they may wish to bring their Bibles. Also tell them participation in verbal prayer is optional, and sentence prayer samples will be provided. They should be encouraged to pray aloud when they're comfortable doing it.

PURPOSE
Have a volunteer read the opening Scripture and the Purpose statement. Comment that David often found himself a fugitive from King Saul and a virtual exile from his own country—surely cause for loneliness! Then share some of your personal experiences with loneliness.

LOOKING INSIDE
Have group members volunteer responses to the three questions. The following information may be used with question 1 as you talk about loneliness at different ages.

Children: Many children are delivered to daycare centers by 7 A.M. and picked up in the evening around 6. Today over 5 million children in America have divorced parents.

Youth: Teenage girls often experience a sense of isolation if they feel unattractive to boys. Failure to meet the expectations of a peer group also results in isolation. Teenage boys, if not caught up in the athletic world of the average high school, often experience anxiety and uncertainty about themselves.

Middle Age: Some men and women feel they have missed life's best opportunities. If they are not at the top of their professions, they can feel set apart from the upwardly mobile. Even if they have arrived at some pinnacle of career success, they may find it truly lonely at the top.

Elderly: They may experience feelings of purposelessness and of not being wanted or needed, especially if they no longer have a mate with whom to share their lives.

AN EPIDEMIC

To open this segment for discussion read the following observations, taken from "Consumer Digest," October, 1986.

> Product Advertising Exploits Loneliness
> More and more people in America are feeling alone, disconnected from the world around them, and many companies are trying to profit from that loneliness, claims author Louise Bernikow.
>
> Bernikow, who wrote "Lonely in America: The Search for Companionship," says that advertisements, such as the "Reach out and touch someone" campaign by AT&T, promise friendships or improved relationships if the consumer uses the advertised product. Bernikow also cities beer commercials by Lowenbrau, Miller, and Coors that depict workers quitting for the day and "developing friendships" while consuming pitcher upon pitcher of beer.
>
> These ads are exploiting a very real problem that many people face—the inability to find or make friends, Bernikow asserts. "The promise of relationships is used to sell alcohol. It's exploitation. They're not selling beer, they're selling friendships," she says.
>
> Bernikow interviewed more than 300 people nationwide and found what she calls an "epidemic" of loneliness among Americans caused by changes in the economy, changes in lifestyles and the family, and an increased mobility.
>
> "Lifetime employment is a vestige of the past," Bernikow says. "The biggest lie in our society is that the company (one works for) is a family. Too many people have worked in the same place for 20 years and then get two hours to clean out their desks."
>
> There is also a link between technology and alienation. Television and videocassette recorders, the personal computer, and automatic teller machines now allow people to do in isolation what used to require human contact to accomplish, Bernikow explains. "The advances in technology

may not cause isolation, but they have made it more possible to live that way."

Have volunteers read the two paragraphs in the study materials. Then identify which of the people describe the four types of loneliness.

- [ ] Circumstantial 2, 4, 5, 6, 7
- [ ] Chosen 1, 3, 7
- [ ] Self-protective 1, 3,
- [ ] Inner-core 4, 7

LONELINESS DEFINED
All the phrases in some way describe the concept of loneliness. Use the responses of participants to stimulate conversation.

CATEGORIES OF LONELINESS
Give participants time to make notations; then as a group discuss the four categories of loneliness, encouraging volunteers to give their examples. The following examples could be added.

Category 1: Circumstantial—Something one can't control, as when others on the job or in our social group fail to include us, by not asking us to join them for lunch or go to a particular activity.

Category 2: Chosen—Because of hurt feelings or misunderstandings, we may withdraw from a group or relationship to avoid hurt. Or it can be that one just doesn't want to engage in an activity, event, type of work, or relationship.

Category 3: Self-protective—May occur in divorce or when a mate dies, when an individual no longer feels comfortable in a group of couples. It is often used as an excuse to avoid relationships.

Category 4: Inner-core—Categories one through three describe external loneliness. Inner-core loneliness is often inexplicable—you are just lonely. Some writers say it has to do with man's sinful nature, and a longing to be in a right relationship with God.

50 LONGING FOR COMPANY

Close this section by polling participants to see which category has the most entries.

BIBLICAL EXAMPLES
The following section gives insight into lonely people in the Bible, and how they handled their feelings.

1. David ultimately trusted in the sovereignty of God during his bouts with loneliness. He may have initially questioned God's intent, but he always bowed to God's will and declared His goodness. David exalts God's faithfulness and pledges his love to Him.

    David shows us that the one absolute way to overcome loneliness is to acknowledge God's sovereignty and put complete trust in Him.

2. The author of Hebrews was assured that because of his position in Christ, God would never leave or forsake him.

    Our personal relationship with the living God through Jesus assures us of triumph over any hurt another person can cause.

3. Paul said he had learned from all his experiences to be content (happy, satisfied, and grateful) in whatever set of circumstances he found himself.

    Another way to overcome loneliness is to thank God for this period in your life. He may be trying to draw you closer to Himself and to make His Word more meaningful in your life. Live daily in the presence of Jesus. Look for changes for the better in your life this week.

4. David was able to see the benefit of his loneliness and other afflictions because they motivated him to better learn God's principles (statutes).

    Another way to overcome loneliness is to use it as a motivation to study and memorize relevant Scripture.

5. Isaiah tells us that God will give continual guidance and protection to those who extend a helping hand to the less fortu-

nate. To those who observe His holy day (the Sabbath) and lead others to do the same, God will provide access to His resources; He will exalt them before other people; and He will provide unending spiritual nourishment.

Another way to overcome loneliness is to look for and seize opportunities to meet other people's physical, social, and emotional needs.

TAKE FIVE
Allow participants five minutes to respond and discuss with a neighbor. The situations listed provide opportunities to review different kinds of loneliness and how they can be overcome. After five minutes, discuss as a group one of these situations — the one that seems most appropriate for your group.

PRAYING TOGETHER
Take about five minutes for prayer. (Time will vary depending on group size.) Praying may be new for participants, so give them permission not to pray aloud until they feel comfortable. Have each group member select a printed prayer, then let each read or say that sentence aloud. As leader, you should pray using only one sentence, modeling the behavior you expect of others.

THIS WEEK
Review the assignment.

LEADER'S NOTES 2
ALONE IN A CROWD

BRIDGE
Bridge from last week's study by asking for volunteers to share lonely moments they experienced during the past week and how they handled each one.

PURPOSE
Have a volunteer read the opening Scripture and the Purpose statement. Give a personal example of how you have experienced loneliness brought on or aggravated by someone else and how with God's help you endured.

LOOKING INSIDE
Invite volunteers to respond to the questions.

STRESSORS
After reviewing the definition for "stressors," follow the instructions for ranking stressors, allowing a few minutes for each individual to fill in the chart with her rankings. Have each list the three highest and lowest. As a group, take time to discuss stressors we handle most of the time, and those we almost never handle.

BIBLICAL "OTHERS"
Have volunteers read the Scriptures, highlighting ways others can create feelings of loneliness:

Psalm 102:8—enemies taunt and use me.
Psalm 88:8—lost closest friends; confined.
2 Timothy 4:16—no support; everyone deserted him.
Matthew 26:56—loss of friends.

RESPONDING IN LOVE
Give a personal example of how applying Matthew 7:12 has blessed you. Discuss each Scripture and the questions following them.

Use the following suggestions to supplement the discussion if needed.

1. Realizing that we all have, to some degree, judgmental natures, we must learn to make conscious efforts to change.

2. Learn to simply and sincerely say "thank you."

3. Realize the critic means well. Understand that only God's judgment counts.

4. Call people by their names. Listen attentively. Spend time with people. Affirm them.

5. Offer a personal testimony on how you've learned to love yourself.

6. To get them started, give a couple of personal examples.

PRAYING TOGETHER
Take about five minutes for prayer. (Time will vary depending on the group size.) Remind participants that they do not have to pray aloud until they feel comfortable. Have the group look at the printed prayers, select one, then begin prayer time.

THIS WEEK
Review the instructions for this week's assignment. Have participants exchange telephone numbers for requesting prayer from one another if the need arises.

LEADER'S NOTES 3
OVERCOMING VERSUS WITHDRAWING

BRIDGE
Bridge from last week's study by inviting volunteers to share their experiences when they prayed to God claiming Jeremiah 33:3 or called a group member to pray on their behalf.

PURPOSE
Have a volunteer read the opening Scripture and the Purpose statement. Point out that our fear of pain can cause us to withdraw in the face of loneliness, rather than to acknowledge it and let God help us overcome it.

LOOKING INSIDE
Allow time for group members to respond to the questions. Add to each from your experience if appropriate.

FEELINGS IDENTIFIED
Read the opening paragraph, then have participants complete the "if only" statements.

Comment: Just as we cannot become younger, neither can we go back in time to a place we have been. God has planned the road ahead. If we focus on the past we become discontent with today and accomplish nothing. It is best to forget our "if onlys." That said, there's nothing wrong with fond memories, so long as we don't depend on them for our life in the present.

Have a volunteer read the next paragraph.

OVERCOMING LONELINESS
Have a volunteer read the paragraph. Give a personal example if you can. Allow participants to discuss their responses to questions which can help in acknowledge loneliness. Ask if they discovered anything new about themselves.

WHEN GOD BRINGS GOOD OUT OF LONELINESS
Have volunteers read the Scriptures about each character. Discuss each as you go.

LEADER'S NOTES   55

1. Joseph could have withdrawn instead of working diligently and earning his master's favor (Genesis 39:1-6); he could have kept silent instead of interpreting dreams (Genesis 40–41); he could have rejected the responsibilities of being second in command (Genesis 41:41-57); he could have pulled away from his family when they were finally reunited (Genesis 42; 45; 47).

   But Joseph realized that it was not his brothers who sent him to Egypt, but God. He also realized that God had sent him to preserve a remnant in the earth for his brothers in order to keep them alive.

   What man meant for evil, God meant for good. God raised Joseph up as a great leader, through his trials, to preserve many lives (Genesis 45:7-8; 50:20).

2. Ruth could have hidden herself away in the house instead of taking the initiative to find food for herself and Naomi (Ruth 2:2); she could have shrunk back from possible rejection by Boaz and possible loss of reputation instead of looking for a kinsman-redeemer (Ruth 3).

   But because she followed her mother-in-law and put herself at risk, Ruth met and married Boaz, and gave birth to Obed, the father of Jesse, the father of David, the forefather of Jesus (Ruth 4:10-17; Matthew 1:5-6).

3. As a result of the lonely circumstances Joseph and Mary endured, Jesus was born in Bethlehem, fulfilling the prophecy of Micah 5:2.

TAKE FIVE
Allow five minutes for participants to discuss their experiences with a neighbor.

PRAYING TOGETHER
Instruct participants to take comfort in the Scriptures. Read them in unison. You may wish to close in a brief prayer for the group.

THIS WEEK
Review the assignment.

LEADER'S NOTES 4
ALONE BUT NOT LONELY

BRIDGE
Check with participants to see, if during the past week, any read a good book, called a friend, wrote a letter, completed a project, or engaged in any activity in response to their loneliness.

PURPOSE
Have a volunteer read the opening Scripture and the Purpose statement. Share your experiences in spending time alone and its value in your life.

LOOKING INSIDE
Have group members share responses to the three questions.

CREATING OPTIONS FOR TIME ALONE
Review the list of activities found in the chart, then allow ample time for participants to rate their responses. When everyone is done, ask group members to list the three activities they most desire to change.

TAKE FIVE
Allow five minutes for participants to discuss with each other how they could make more time for the three activities listed.

BENEFITS OF TIME ALONE
Have participants read the Scriptures and complete the sentences. Provide the following examples as needed, but assure group members that there is not one right response; allow them to personalize each of these benefit statements.

- ☐ Time alone allows for rest.
- ☐ Time alone allows one to learn new things.
- ☐ Time alone allows you to become sensitive to others.
- ☐ Time alone allows for personal growth.
- ☐ Time alone allows for a relationship with God.

As you discuss each passage and its sentence completion, ask:

LEADER'S NOTES 57

- [ ] In what specific ways would this be a benefit?
- [ ] When have you felt a strong need for this benefit?
- [ ] What would you need to do to use your time alone for this end?
- [ ] Which benefit(s) would you most like to incorporate into your life, starting this week?
- [ ] How will you do it?

Take plenty of time to draw out specific, creative, and constructive ideas.

PRAYING TOGETHER
Take time for prayer. Have participants select one of the printed prayers or write their own.

THIS WEEK
Review the assignment.

LEADER'S NOTES 5
LONELY PLACES

BRIDGE
Review last week's assignment, then ask whether anyone would like to share a journal entry.

PURPOSE
Have a volunteer read the opening Scripture and the Purpose statement aloud.

LOOKING INSIDE
Allow participants to "look inside" themselves, to share their lonely places and who was there to comfort them. Ask volunteers to describe a lonely place they remember as a positive experience. You may want to begin with an example.

LONELY THOUGHTS
Discuss lonely places, lonely thoughts, and how we usually handle them. Allow each individual to respond to the list of lonely thoughts, marking those they have and have not experienced. When they have completed this, ask if anyone has additions to the list. Review the example of overcoming an event. Then allow time for participants to select one item from their list and note how they might overcome it. Allow several to share, as time permits.

LEAH'S LONELY PLACE
Have volunteers read the summarized story of Jacob, Leah, and Rachel. When you come to the questions, answer as a group.

- ☐ List Leah's emotions. Some responses could include unloved, rejected, lonely, abandoned, forsaken, worthless.
- ☐ What did Leah need and want? Among the possible responses are love, comfort, attention, and acceptance.
- ☐ What was God's response? He allowed Leah to bear a son. In those days it was a great honor to bear children, and Leah would bear many for Jacob.
- ☐ What is the difference between Leah's response to the birth of her first son and her fourth? Leah finally accepted

the situation, one she couldn't change. She praised God for His provision for her. This wasn't easy for Leah, and it's not easy for us. Where there is great pain, the hurt and loneliness can be overwhelming. But God understands what we are experiencing.

TAKE FIVE
Allow time for group members to share what they have gained from these verses. Help them recognize that God's predetermined plan is for us all to be conformed to the image of His Son. He has promised those who love Him that He will cause all things to work together for good. Our response is to be love, trust, and obedience.

OUR RESPONSE
Discuss how we are to respond or act in the midst of stress, loneliness, and change. Have volunteers read the Scriptures and draw out responses. Use the following suggestions if needed.

Genesis 6:22—Obedience

1 Thessalonians 5:16-18—Rejoice always; pray without ceasing; in everything give thanks

James 1:2-4—Consider trials a joy; know that the testing of your faith produces endurance.

Philippians 4:6—Do not be anxious; let your requests be known to God by prayer.

Philippians 4:8—Focus on whatever is true, honorable, right, pure, lovely, of good repute, excellent, anything worthy of praise.

PRAYING TOGETHER
Take time for group prayer. If you haven't held hands in a circle for prayer, do so at this time.

THIS WEEK
Review the assignment.

LEADER'S NOTES 6
GETTING BY WITH A LITTLE HELP FROM MY FRIEND

BRIDGE
Ask volunteers to give examples from their "Lonely Thoughts" list, and what they wrote about overcoming the feelings or situations. Ask whether they could do anything about the situations. Were they able to accept the outcomes?

PURPOSE
Have a volunteer read the opening Scripture and the Purpose statement. You may want to comment: We all need friends who care and listen, who are with us in times of need, sorrow, and joy. Yet there are many in our cities who are lonely and without friends. Are we sensitive to them? Scripture pictures Christ as compassionate and caring, One who deeply cares about the needs and hurts of every individual, One who will never fail or forsake us.

LOOKING INSIDE
These questions are deeply personal for some. While you want to encourage openness, be careful not to press too deeply for public responses. The last part of question 2 may be rephrased, "What special character traits are found in a friend?" Responses may include: trustworthiness, honesty, unconditional acceptance, giving, caring, etc.

FRIENDS
Since the full accounts of these friendships are not printed in the participants' copies, you may want to read some of the following Scripture on this section. The character traits given here are only a few of the possible answers.

1. Jonathan risked the anger of his father by standing up for David when David's life was in danger. Characteristics: loving, giving, accepting, trustworthy (1 Samuel 18:1-4; 19:1-7; 20:1-17).

2. Friends of the paralytic: determined, faithful, persistent (Luke 5:17-26).

3. Mary risked her own reputation to express her love for Jesus at a time very close to His death. Characteristics: giving, generous, loving, determined (not influenced by others' opinions) (John 12:1-8).

OPTIONAL — MORE BIBLICAL FRIENDS

If your group would like to look at more examples of friends from Scripture, use these characters.

1. Abram and Lot (Genesis 14:1-16). Lot was in the wrong place at the wrong time and was taken captive by the warring kings. Abram risked his life to rescue Lot from the enemy forces. Characteristics: present in time of need and willing to help at any cost; faithful.

2. Nathan and David (2 Samuel 12:1-13). The Prophet Nathan confronted King David with his sins of adultery and murder. A true friend is one who will lovingly rebuke, and then will be there during the healing and recovery process. Characteristics: honest, trustworthy, faithful, encouraging.

THE ULTIMATE FRIEND

Together, list some of the character traits you've identified in the human friends, and talk about ways Jesus exhibits those same traits. Use the following examples to trigger ideas if needed, but encourage participants to give personal examples from their relationship with Jesus if they feel comfortable. You can model that openness by giving examples from your own life.

- ☐ Loving: He so loved us that, while we were still sinners, He died for us.
- ☐ Giving, generous: Gave not only His life, but the Holy Spirit, the gifts of the Spirit, eternal life, peace, and more.
- ☐ Accepting: As shown in His dealings with Zaccheus, the Samaritan woman, the woman caught in adultery — and us!
- ☐ Trustworthy: His promises are true.
- ☐ Determined: Will not let us go, no matter how hard the devil tries to take us away.

In the account from Luke, Jesus encounters a man suffering with leprosy, a painful, progressive, incurable disease that resulted in disfigurement and often death. Those suffering from the disease were ostracized by family, friends, and community, and were required to live in colonies. Their emotional problems were as severe as their physical pain, for when they suffered, they lacked support from family and friends. One man, apparently in the final and most painful stage of the disease, approached Jesus in faith. According to levitical law, the man should not have come closer than 100 feet. Yet Jesus reached out and touched him; and because of the man's faith and Christ's compassion, he was healed and returned to his home and family.

The leper's basic needs were to be healed physically, emotionally, and spiritually. Jesus reached out to him and provided that healing.

TAKE FIVE
Allow participants five minutes (or more, if appropriate) to discuss with their neighbor the needs in each other's lives.

PRAYING TOGETHER
The Bible contains many promises for God's children. All we need to do is appropriate them in our lives. Use each of the Scriptures in your prayer time; let volunteers read one each, or read them in unison.

After you read John 3:16 and Romans 5:8, comment that God's provision for man's most basic need is the gift of His only Son, that we might have eternal life. With these promises of God, why do we continue to ignore the power and victory He wants for each of us?

THIS WEEK
After reviewing the assignment for this week, have each participant turn to "Five Steps for Accepting Jesus Christ as Your Personal Lord and Savior," found at the back of the book. Review it and encourage group members to spend time working through it.

CLOSING
Provide the words to any of the songs listed in the study and sing them together as a group.

FIVE STEPS FOR ACCEPTING JESUS CHRIST AS YOUR PERSONAL LORD AND SAVIOR

"For God so loved the world, that He gave His one and only Son, that whoever believes in Him shall not perish but have eternal life" *(John 3:16)*.

ACTION	SCRIPTURE	PRAYER	BENEFITS
1. ADMIT your need	Romans 3:23 Romans 6:23	Acknowledge you are a sinner	Eternal life
2. RECOGNIZE the provision	Romans 5:8 Romans 5:19	Acknowledge Christ died on the cross for you	Provides for your needs
3. ACCEPT forgiveness	Acts 3:19 Ephesians 2:8	Say you are sorry for your old ways and receive forgiveness	Eternal forgiveness
4. INVITE Christ into your life	Romans 10:13	Invite Christ into your heart	Continued relationship in prayer with a living God
5. COMMIT your life to Him	1 Peter 1:2 1 Peter 4:19 2 John 1:6 Psalm 37:4-5	Express your willingness to live for Christ, ask for His help to grow in your knowledge and understanding of Him and His will for your life	Obedience and a disciplined life with Christ will carry over to your personal and work life

DATE OF YOUR SPIRITUAL BIRTHDAY _____

GOD'S GIFTS TO YOU	SCRIPTURE	PRAYER	BENEFITS
HOLY SPIRIT	John 14:14-18, 26 Hebrews 13:6 1 Corinthians 12:4 Matthew 7:11 Galatians 5:22	Thank God for the gift of the Spirit	Comforter Helper Giver of Gifts Fruit of the Spirit
HIS PROMISES	2 Peter 1:3-4 2 Corinthians 12:9 Isaiah 40:31 James 1:5-8 1 John 1:7 Psalm 121:7-8 Isaiah 26:3-4	Ask Christ to reveal all things that are good and pure Give thanks for this special day	Security Power Strength Wisdom Fellowship Preservation Peace